Wild Weather

Hail

by Julie Murray

UYZ207
268.0 kts 9874 ft

VVW
307.2

OMH
302.9 kts 8094 ft

Dash!
LEVELED READERS

3

Dash!
LEVELED READERS

Level 1 – Beginning
Short and simple sentences with familiar words or patterns for children who are beginning to understand how letters and sounds go together.

Level 2 – Emerging
Longer words and sentences with more complex language patterns for readers who are practicing common words and letter sounds.

Level 3 – Transitional
More developed language and vocabulary for readers who are becoming more independent.

abdopublishing.com
Published by Abdo Zoom, a division of ABDO, P.O. Box 398166, Minneapolis, Minnesota 55439.
Copyright © 2018 by Abdo Consulting Group, Inc. International copyrights reserved in all countries.
No part of this book may be reproduced in any form without written permission from the publisher.

Printed in the United States of America, North Mankato, Minnesota.
092017
012018

Photo Credits: iStock, Shutterstock, ©ERZ / CC BY-SA 3.0 p. 14-15
Production Contributors: Kenny Abdo, Jennie Forsberg, Grace Hansen, John Hansen
Design Contributors: Dorothy Toth, Christina Doffing

Publisher's Cataloging in Publication Data
Names: Murray, Julie, author.
Title: Hail / by Julie Murray.
Description: Minneapolis, Minnesota: Abdo Zoom, 2018. | Series: Wild weather |
    Includes online resource and index.
Identifiers: LCCN 2017939262 | ISBN 9781532120879 (lib.bdg.) | ISBN 9781532121999 (ebook) |
    ISBN 9781532122552 (Read-to-Me ebook)
Subjects: LCSH: Hail--Juvenile literature. | Weather--Juvenile literature. | Environment--Juvenile
    literature.
Classification: DDC 551.5781--dc23
LC record available at https://lccn.loc.gov/2017939262

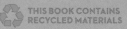

Table of Contents

Hail

Ping! Ping! Clunk! What is that loud sound?

It's hail bouncing off the roof! Luckily, you're safe inside. You don't want to be outside during a hailstorm.

Hail is a ball of ice. It forms during thunderstorms.

Hail can be as small as a pea or as big as a softball.

How It Forms

Hail forms in storm clouds that are filled with water droplets and wind.

Water falls and the wind pushes the droplets up to the tops of the clouds. It is cold up there and the drops get an icy coating.

The balls of ice fall back down and the wind pushes them up again. They bounce around like ping pong balls.

Each time they go to the tops
of the clouds, they get another
layer of ice.

Eventually, the ice balls become too heavy for the wind to blow them back up. They fall to the ground as hailstones.

Hail falls fast from the sky.
Baseball size hail can travel
90 mph (144 kph)!

You can cut open a hailstone and see how many times it made it to the tops of the clouds.

Each ring is another layer of ice that was added. Some hail has just a few layers, but others have many.

Hail Damage

Hail only lasts a few minutes, but the **damage** can be great. It can break windows and ruin roofs.

It can dent cars and destroy farm **crops**. Some farm crops are wiped out from a hailstorm in just a few minutes.

Hail usually occurs during the warm months of spring and summer. Once on the ground, hail melts fast.

In big hailstorms, hail can cover the ground. It can look like it snowed outside!

Meteorologists use radars, satellites, and **weather balloons** to track weather systems. These tools allow them to **predict** when and where hail will fall.

Hail can cause injury to people too, so be sure to get inside if hail is heading your way!

More Facts

- In 1980, Orient, Iowa, had one of the biggest hailstorms ever. The hail drifts were six feet (1.8 m) high!

- The largest hailstone recorded fell in South Dakota in 2010. It was eight inches (20 cm) across and weighed almost two pounds (0.9 kg).

- Hail causes $1 billion in **damage** in the US each year. This includes property damage and **crop** loss.

Glossary

crops – plants grown on a farm.

damage – harm that makes something less useful or valuable.

predict – say that a specified thing will happen in the future.

weather balloon – a balloon used to carry instruments into the sky to gather meteorological data in the atmosphere.

Index

Online Resources

Booklinks
NONFICTION NETWORK
FREE! ONLINE NONFICTION RESOURCES

To learn more about hail, please visit **abdobooklinks.com**. These links are routinely monitored and updated to provide the most current information available.